BOOMER GIRL

Other Books by Cathy Hamilton

Momisms

Dadisms

Kidisms

Mom's the Word

Dadgummit

The Girlfriends' Bible

The Girlfriends' Bible on Dating, Mating, and Other Matters of the Flesh

I Love You More Than Beer (with Rex Hamilton)

BOOMER GiRL

Fighting Midlife One Crisis at a Time

CATHY HAMILTON

Andrews McMeel
Publishing, LLC

Kansas City

Boomer Girl: Fighting Midlife One Crisis at a Time copyright © 2007 by Ms. Communications. All rights reserved. Printed in China. No part of this book may be used or reproduced in any manner whatsoever without written permission except in the case of reprints in the context of reviews. For information, write Andrews McMeel Publishing, LLC, an Andrews McMeel Universal company, 4520 Main Street, Kansas City, Missouri 64111.

07 08 09 10 11 WKT 10 9 8 7 6 5 4 3 2 1

ISBN-13: 978-0-7407-6170-6
ISBN-10: 0-7407-6170-6

Library of Congress Control Number: 2006933024

ATTENTION: SCHOOLS AND BUSINESSES

Andrews McMeel books are available at quantity discounts with bulk purchase for educational, business, or sales promotional use. For information, please write to: Special Sales Department, Andrews McMeel Publishing, LLC, 4520 Main Street, Kansas City, Missouri 64111.

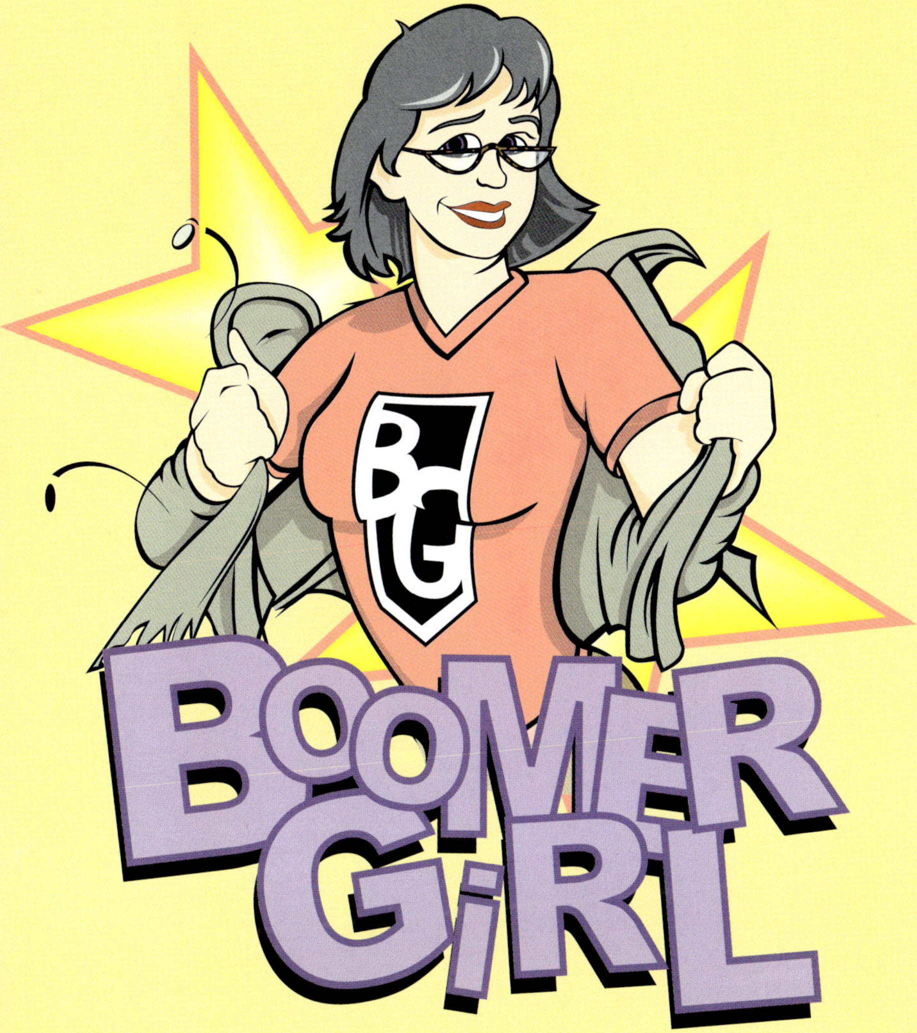
BG
BOOMER GIRL

Faster than a raging mood swing . . .

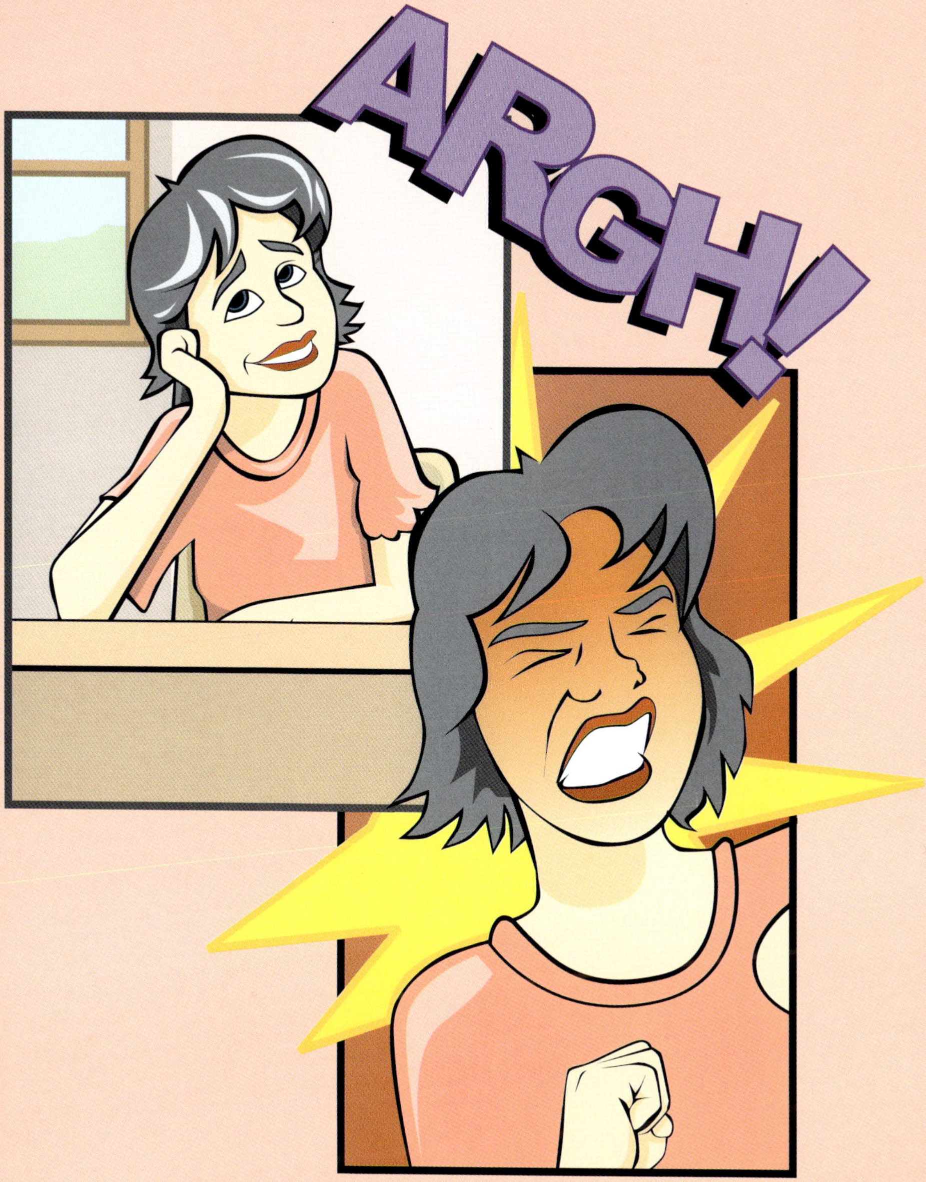
ARGH!

More powerful than +3.0 reading glasses...

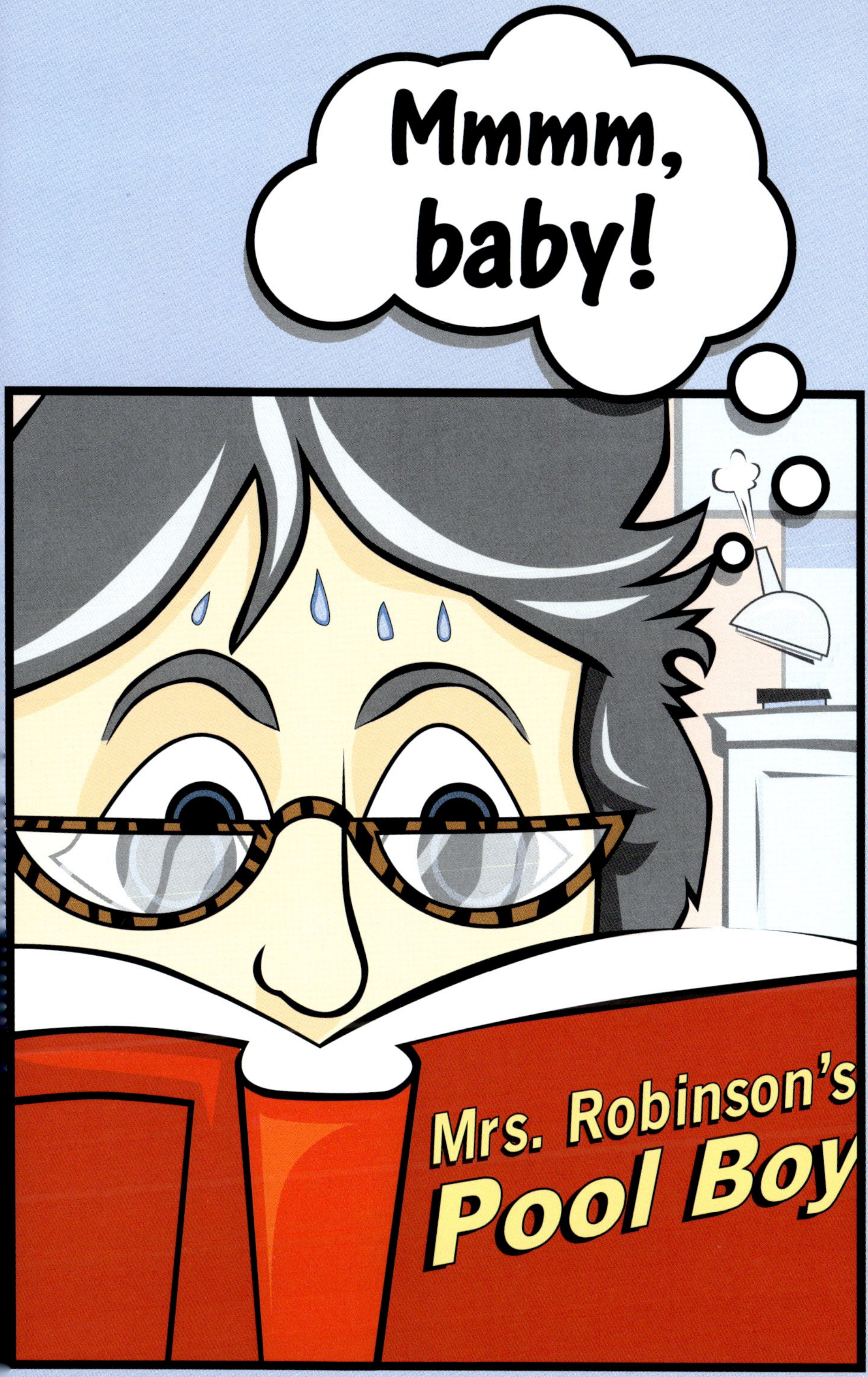
Mmmm, baby!
Mrs. Robinson's Pool Boy

Able to sleep five hours in a single night . . .

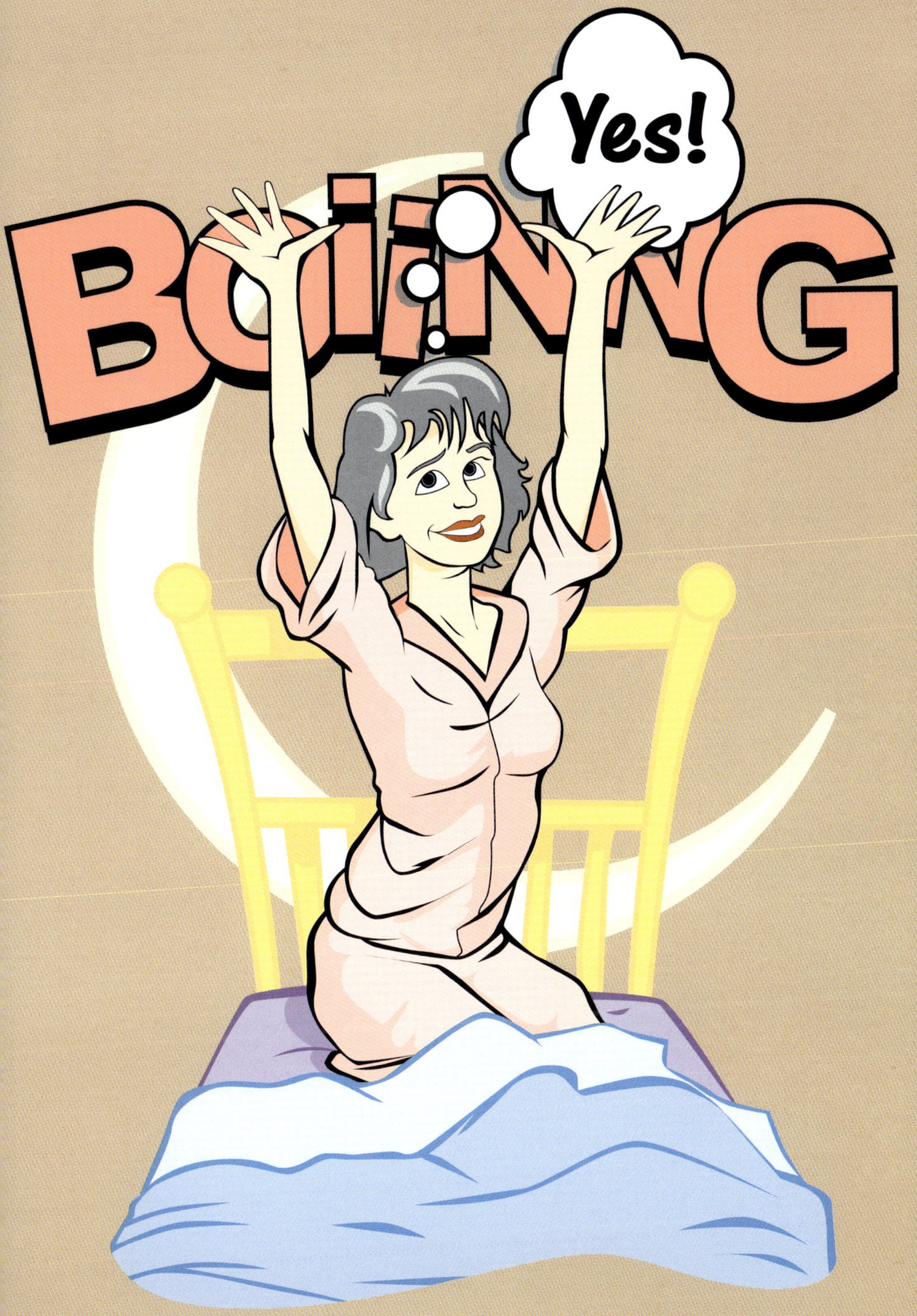
Yes!
BOiiNNG

**Look! Up in the sky . . .
she's a blur!**

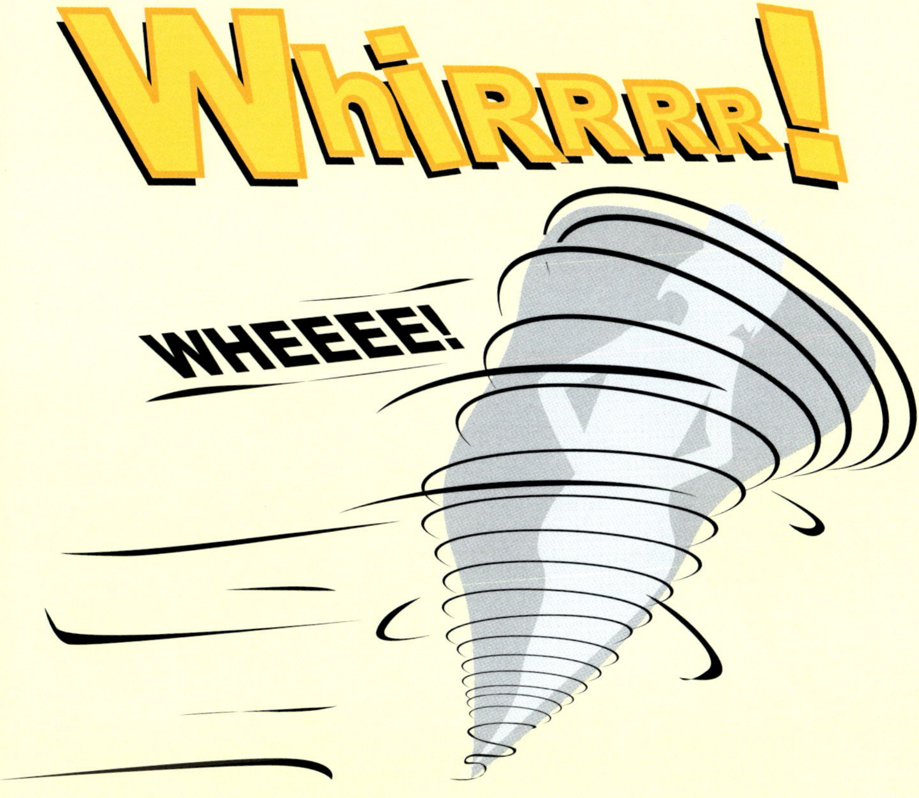
WHIRRRR!
WHEEEE!

She's insane!

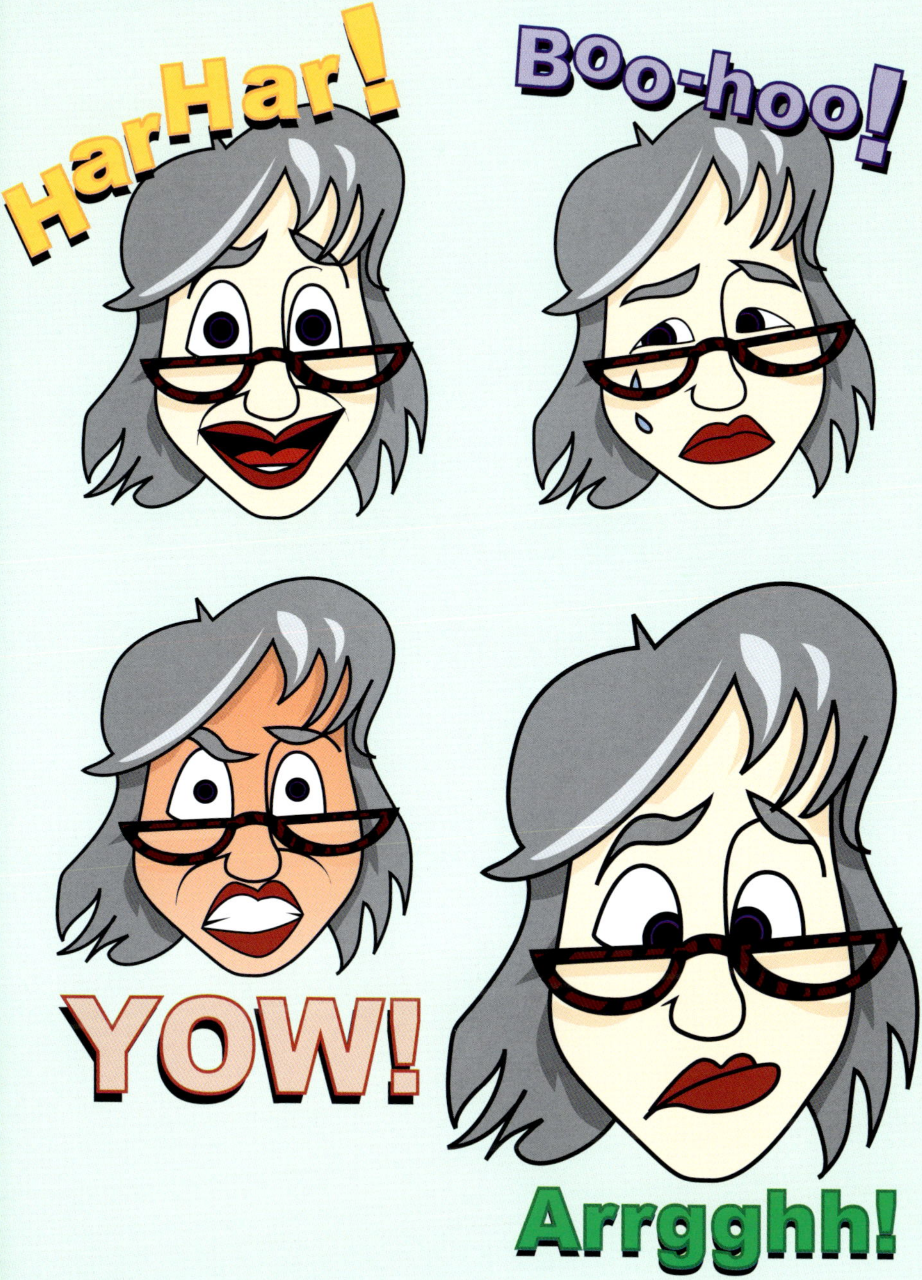
HarHar!
Boo-hoo!
YOW!
Arrgghh!

She's Boomer Girl!

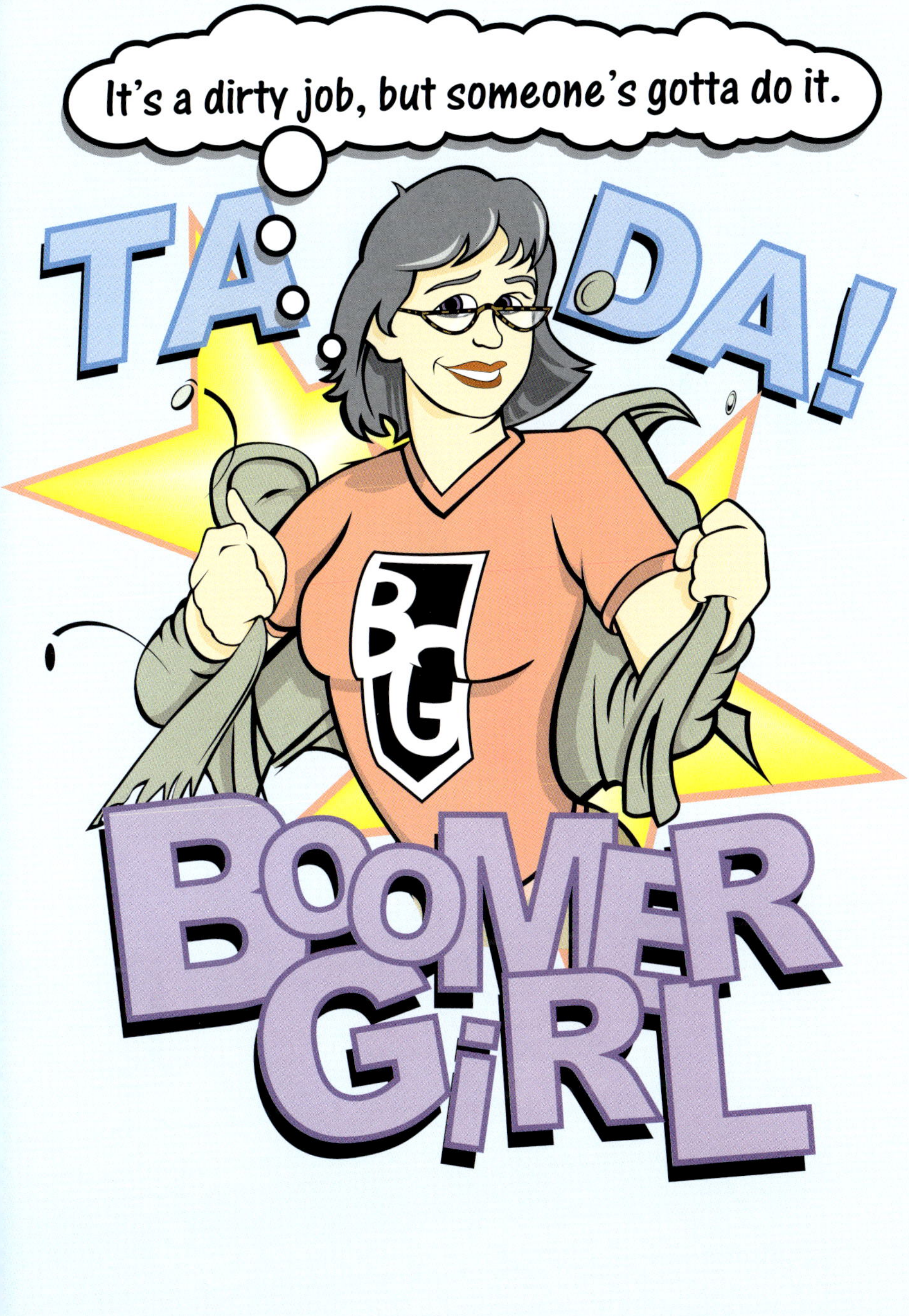
It's a dirty job, but someone's gotta do it.
TA-DA!
BG
BOOMER GIRL

Mornings are no
match for Boomer Girl.
A fantastic multitasker,
she has mastered
the art of doing
ten things at once.

Sell at $85 a share! Oh. Sorry, Mom, I must've misdialed.
TWWINNG!
SCHWOOP!
WHISH!

With superhuman efficiency, Boomer Girl saves valuable time by striking three yoga poses at once and still manages to breathe!

Focus. Find your center. Did I start the dishwasher last night? Focus! Where'd I put my glasses? Focus, dammit!

Boomer Girl refuses to live and die by a stupid number on a scale . . . particularly when that number is three digits higher than it was yesterday!

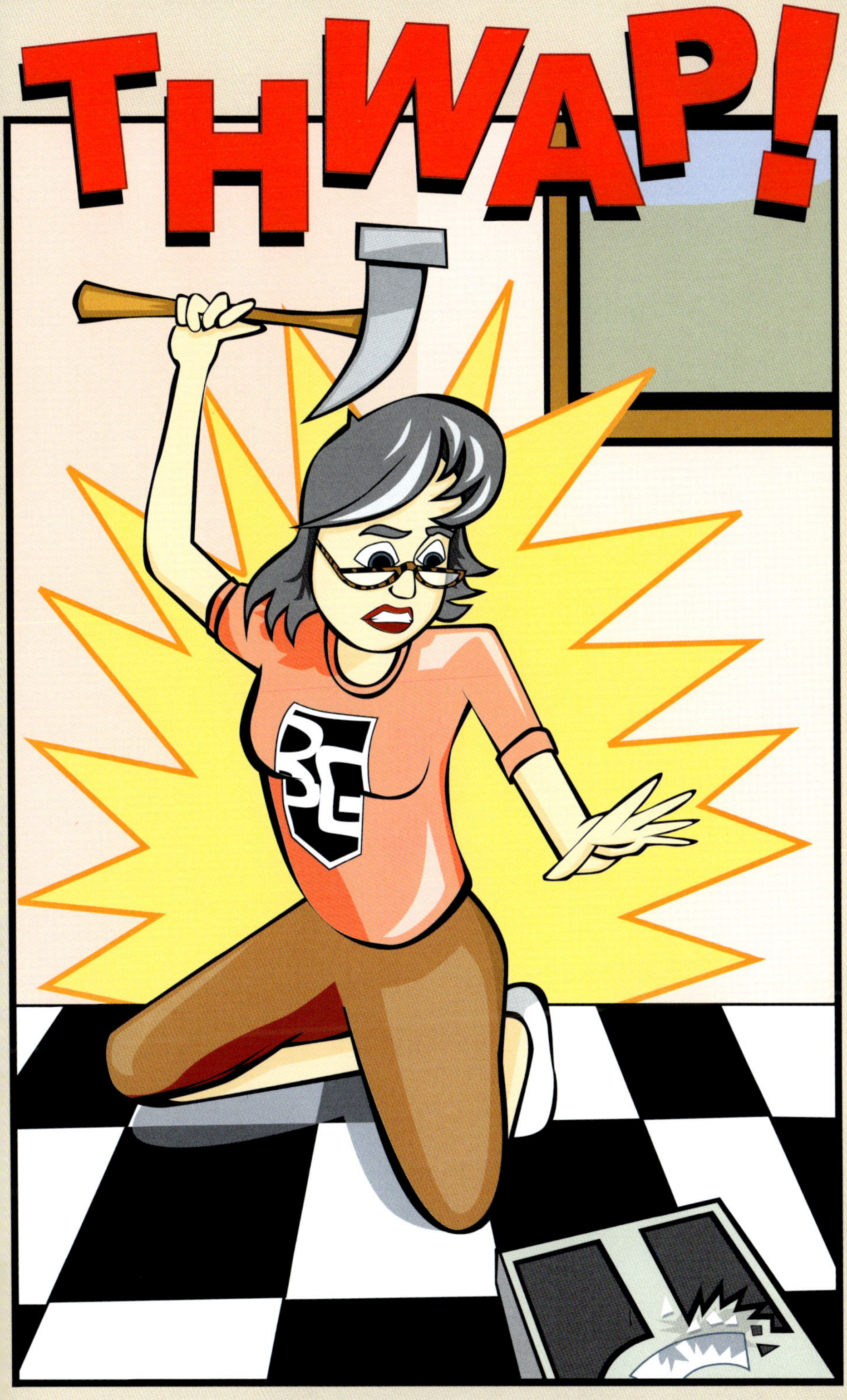
THWAP!
BG

Multivitamin . . .
soy supplement . . .
calcium . . .
fish oil . . . ginseng . . .
antidepressant.
Boomer Girl is ready
to take on the day!

Prozac
Ginseng
Vita-Woman
Calcium
Didn't I take these an hour ago?
GULP!
GULP!
GULP!

Out the door by 7:30 a.m., Boomer Girl is on schedule to conquer the world!

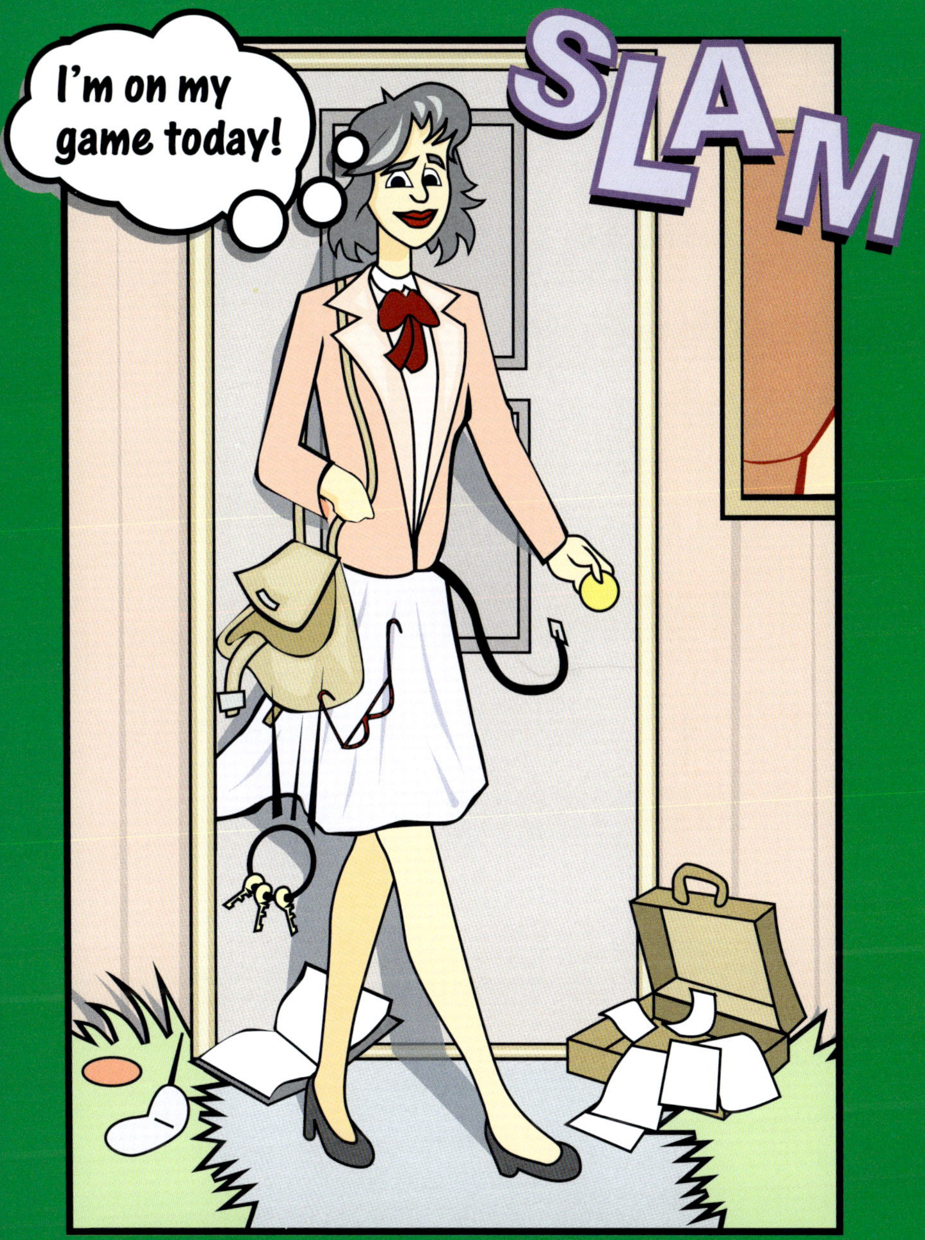
I'm on my game today!
SLAM

Carl the Evil Car Mechanic, seriously misjudging Boomer Girl's mood, informs her that the repair cost will be double the original estimate.

GRRiiPPP!
Damn straight, you'll make it right. Or I'll rip the gaskets from your cylinder head!

**With no regards for
her personal safety
or the kink in her neck,
Boomer Girl checks out
the young talent
on the street.**

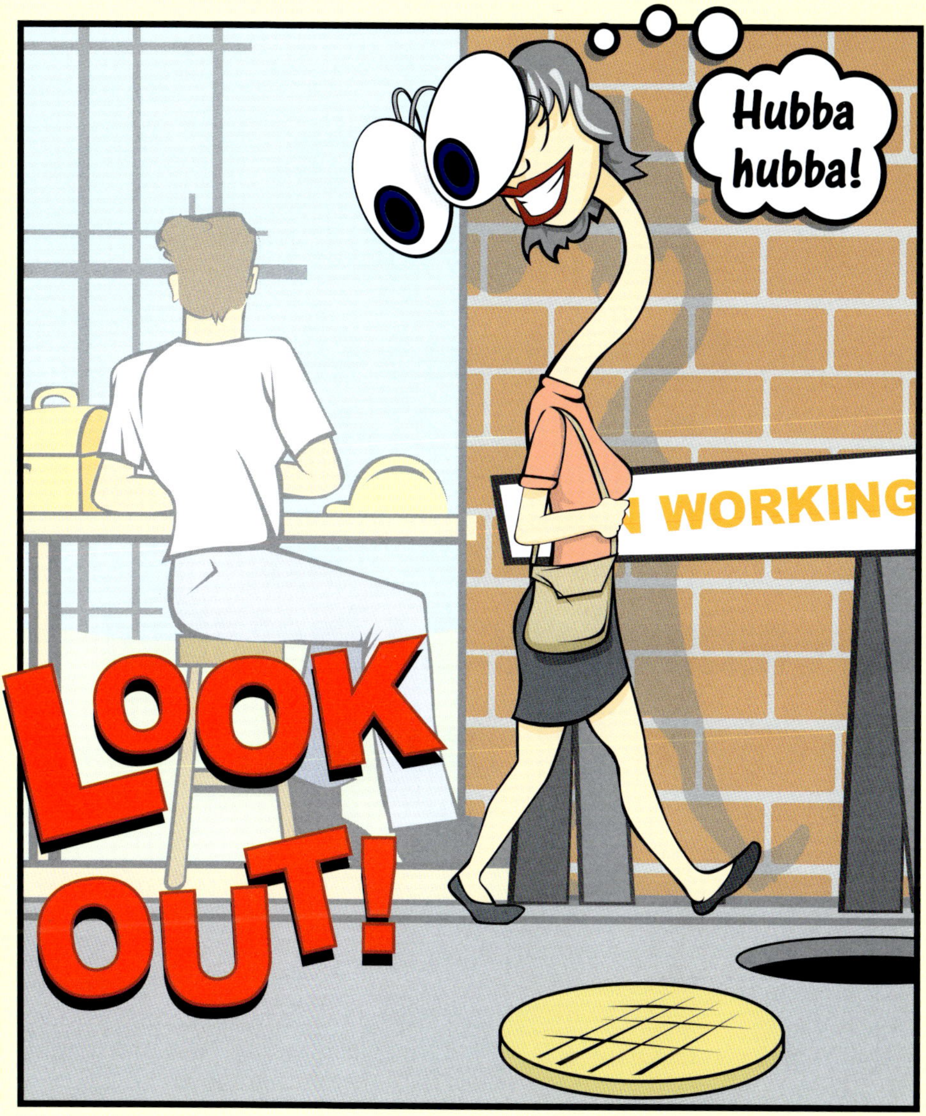
Hubba hubba!
N WORKING
LOOK OUT!

At the office, her menopausal co-workers cheer Boomer Girl for demanding that ceiling fans be installed in the building.

STRIKE!

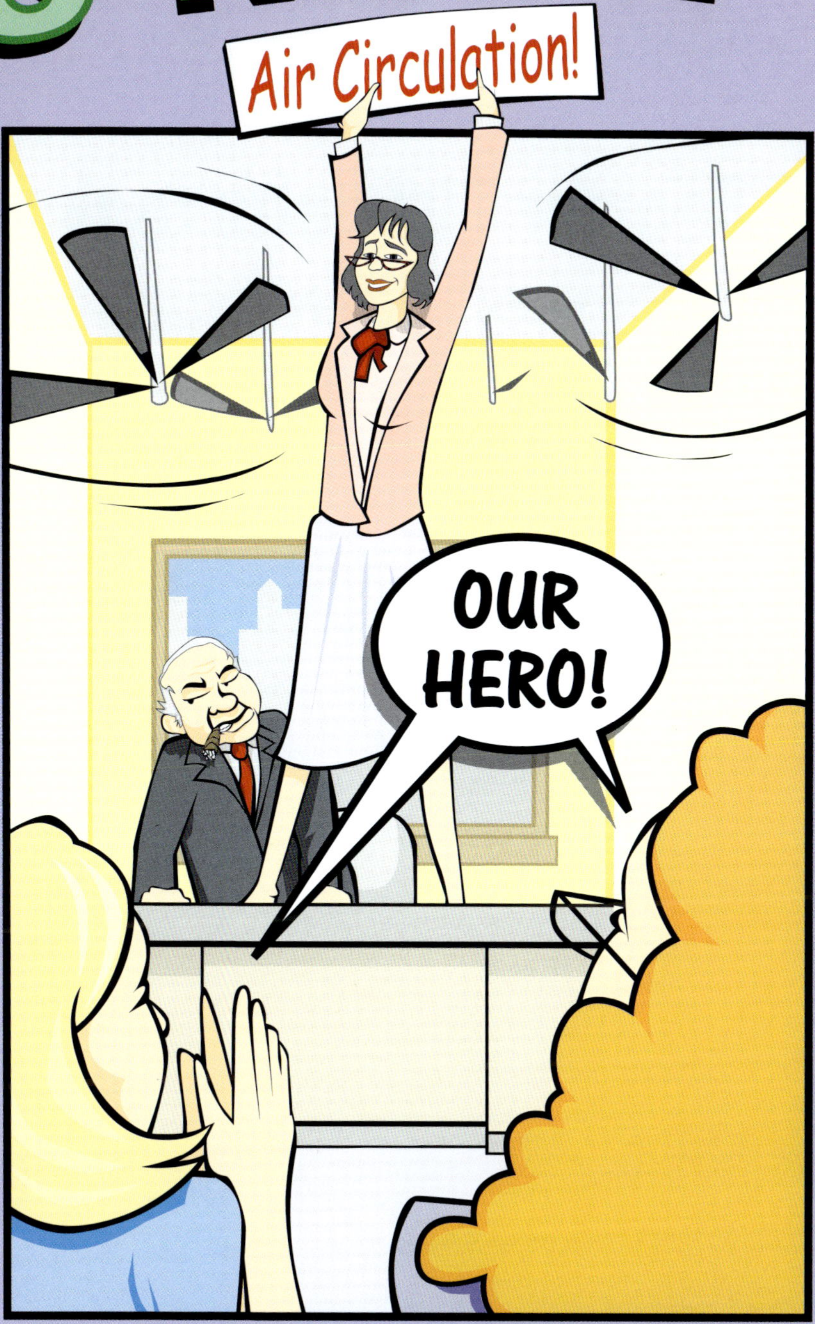

Boomer Girl bolts to the restroom, destroying all obstacles in her path, as nature's call quickly turns into a five-alarm emergency.

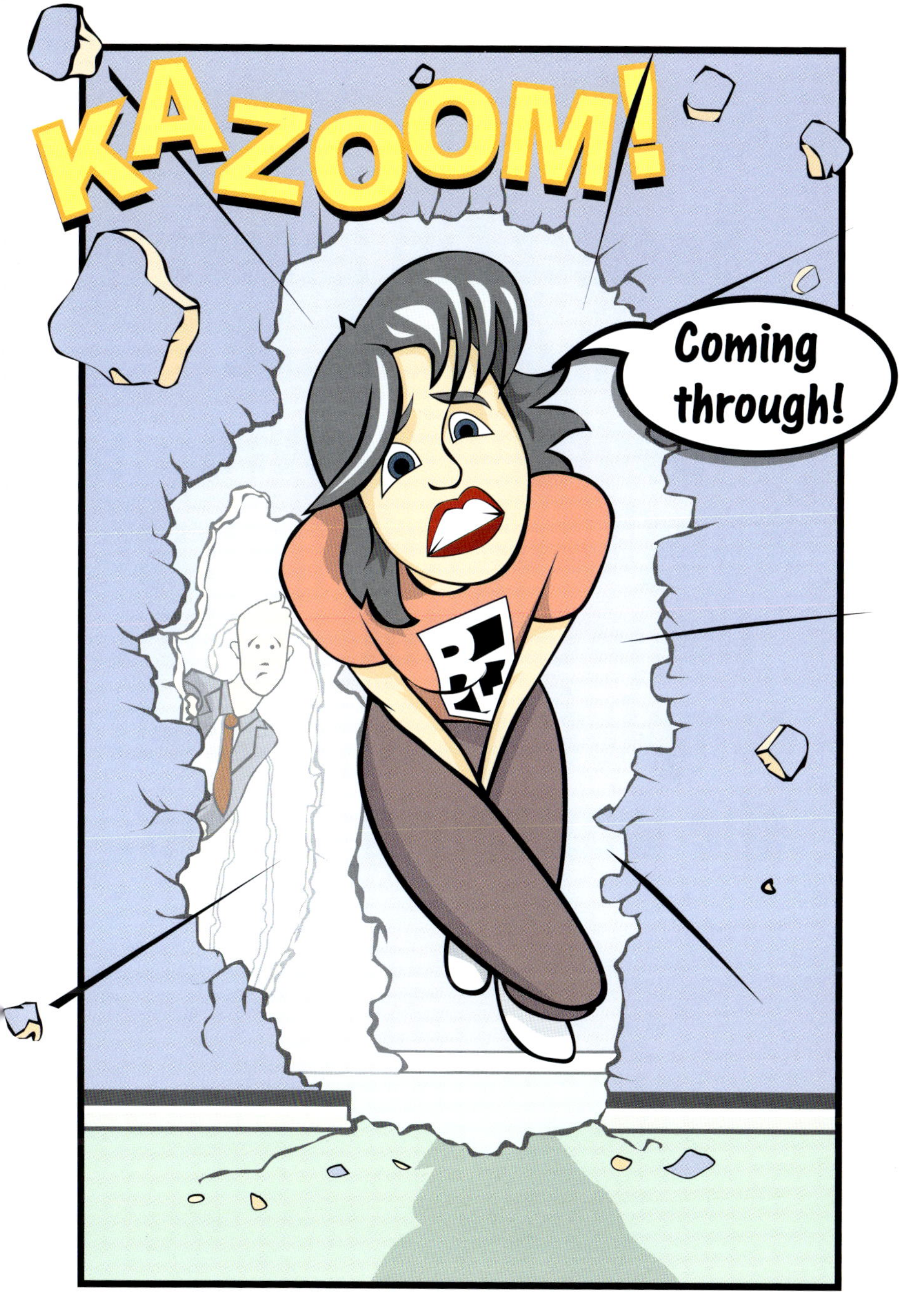
KAZOOM!
Coming through!

Boomer Girl knocks 'em dead in the boardroom, even though halfway through the presentation she completely forgot what she was talking about.

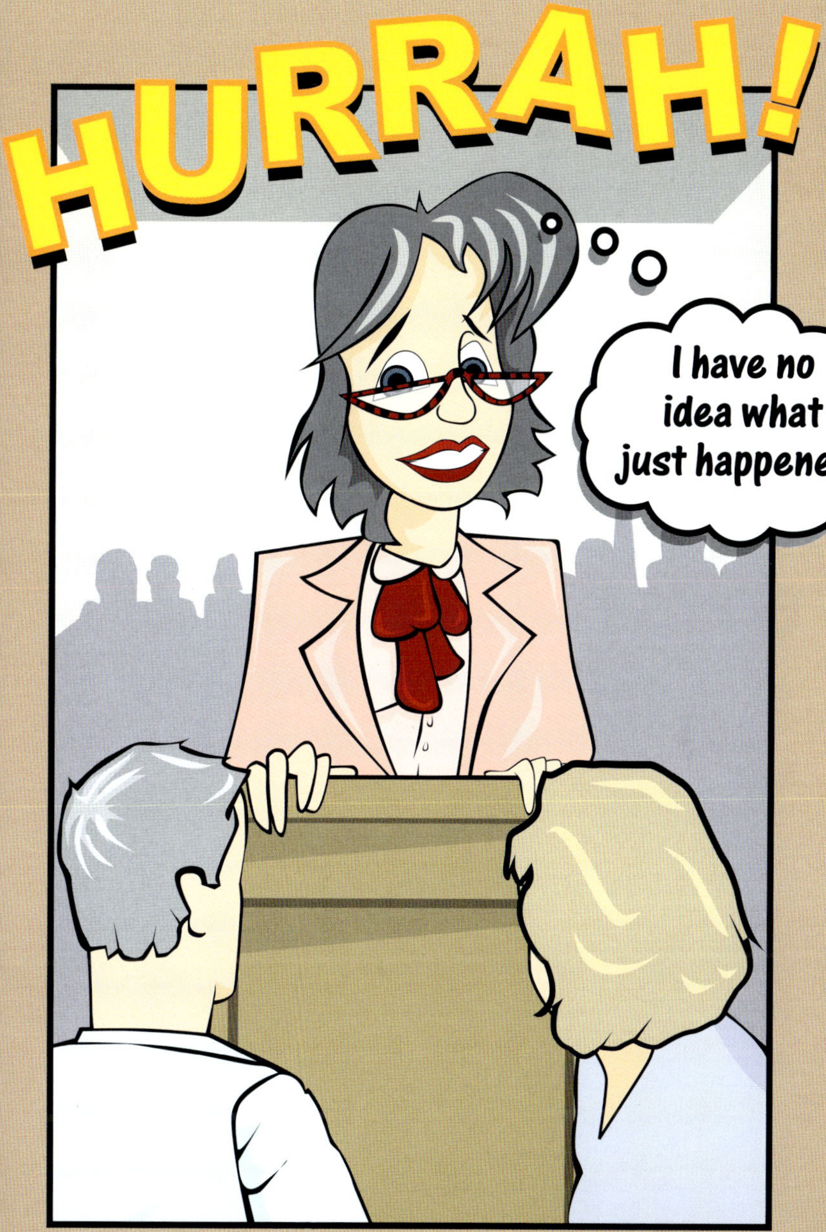
HURRAH!
I have no idea what just happened.

Hot flashes aren't a bummer for Boomer Girl . . . just a great excuse to show off her sexy underwear!

RRRiPP!

As a role model, Boomer Girl is a champion for good nutrition. That's why she always makes sure to eat from all five food groups.

I'll take one Irish Cream, a raspberry, one hot chili pepper, pumpkin spice, and coconut!

Boomer Girl:
Fighting for youth, gusto, and the American Express card!

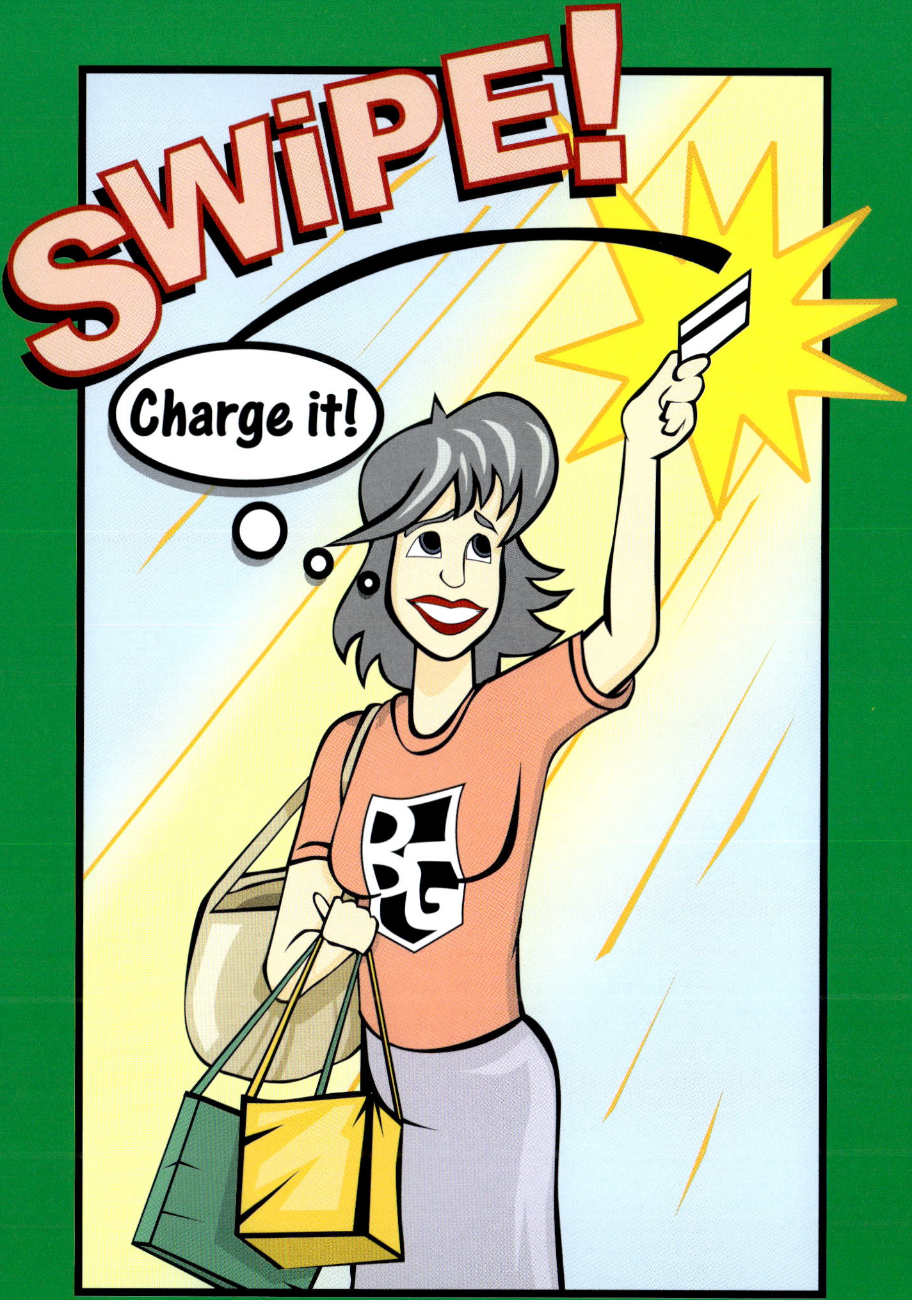
SWiPE!
Charge it!

Boomer Girl fights the good fight when it really counts.

SHOE SALE!
SHOE SALE!
SHOE SALE!
Now THAT was a job for Boomer Girl!
KA-CHING!

Boomer Girl makes mincemeat of lying, no-good salespeople who will say anything to earn a commission.

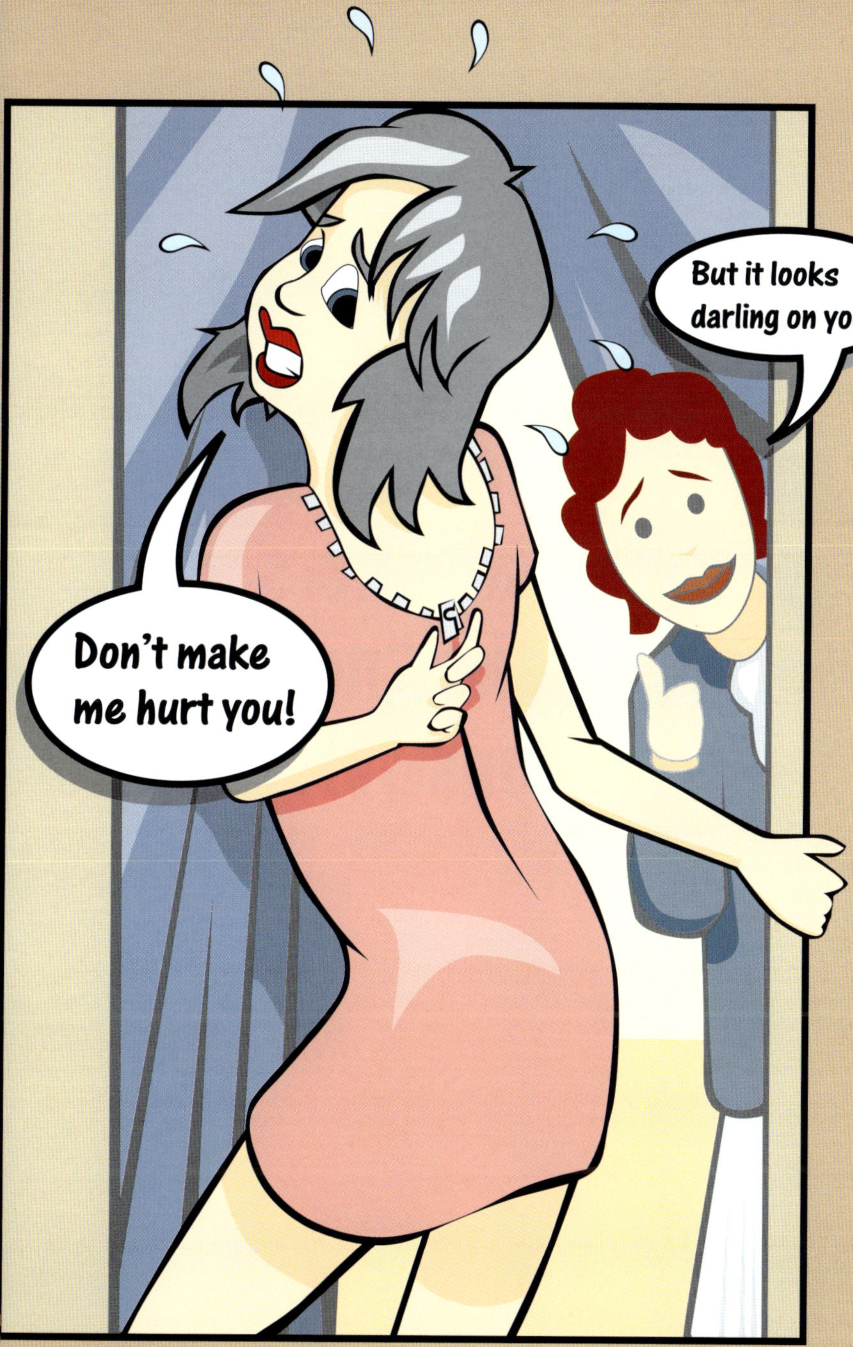
But it looks darling on you!
Don't make me hurt you!

Boomer Girl has no patience for diabolical perfume squirters who won't take "no" for an answer!

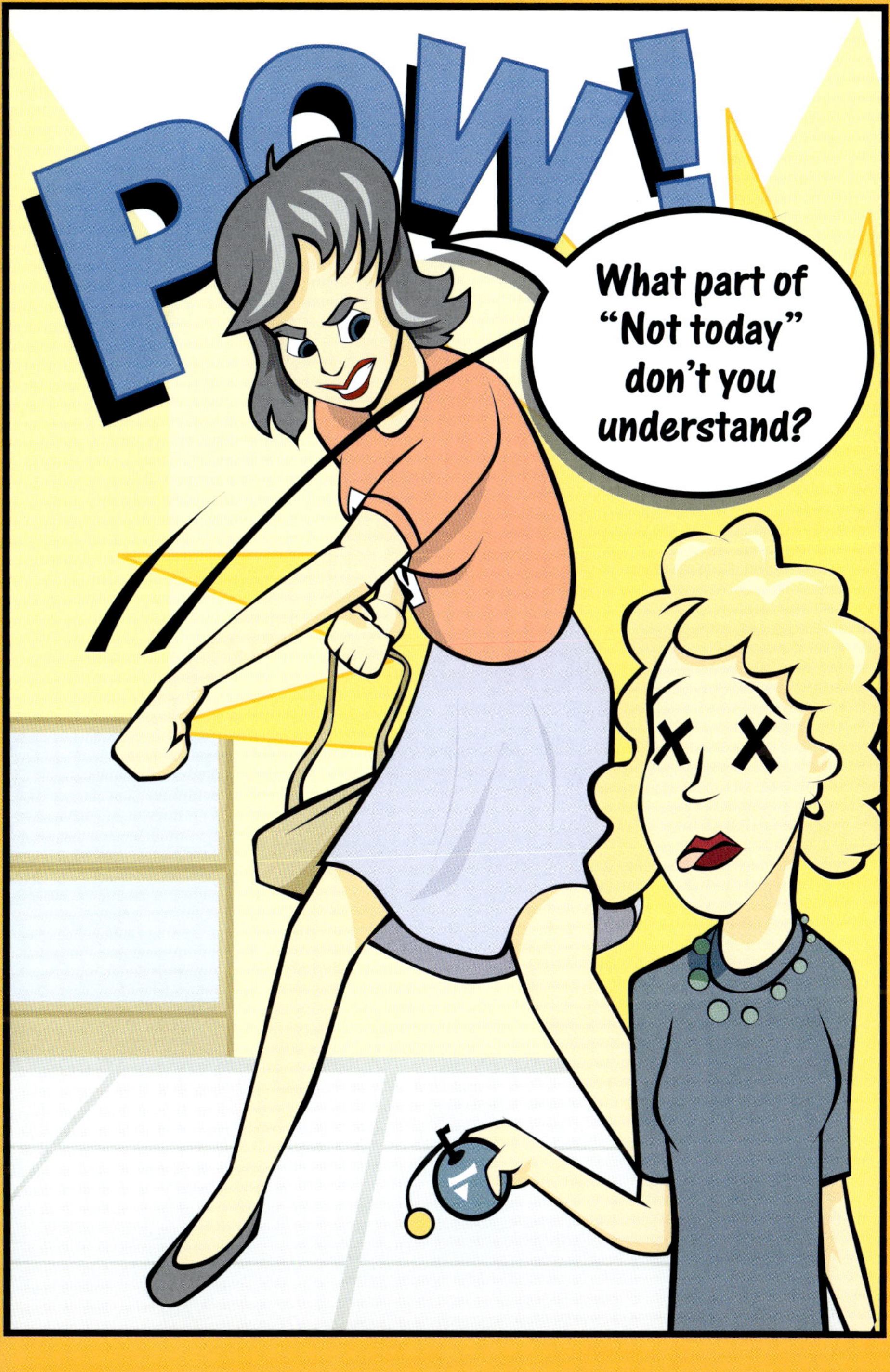
POW!
What part of "Not today" don't you understand?

Boomer Girl's ingenuity knows no bounds when it comes to finding a good spot for a power nap!

BEDDING SALE TODAY!

A natural chameleon, Boomer Girl conceals her identity to ward off the evil forces in her world.

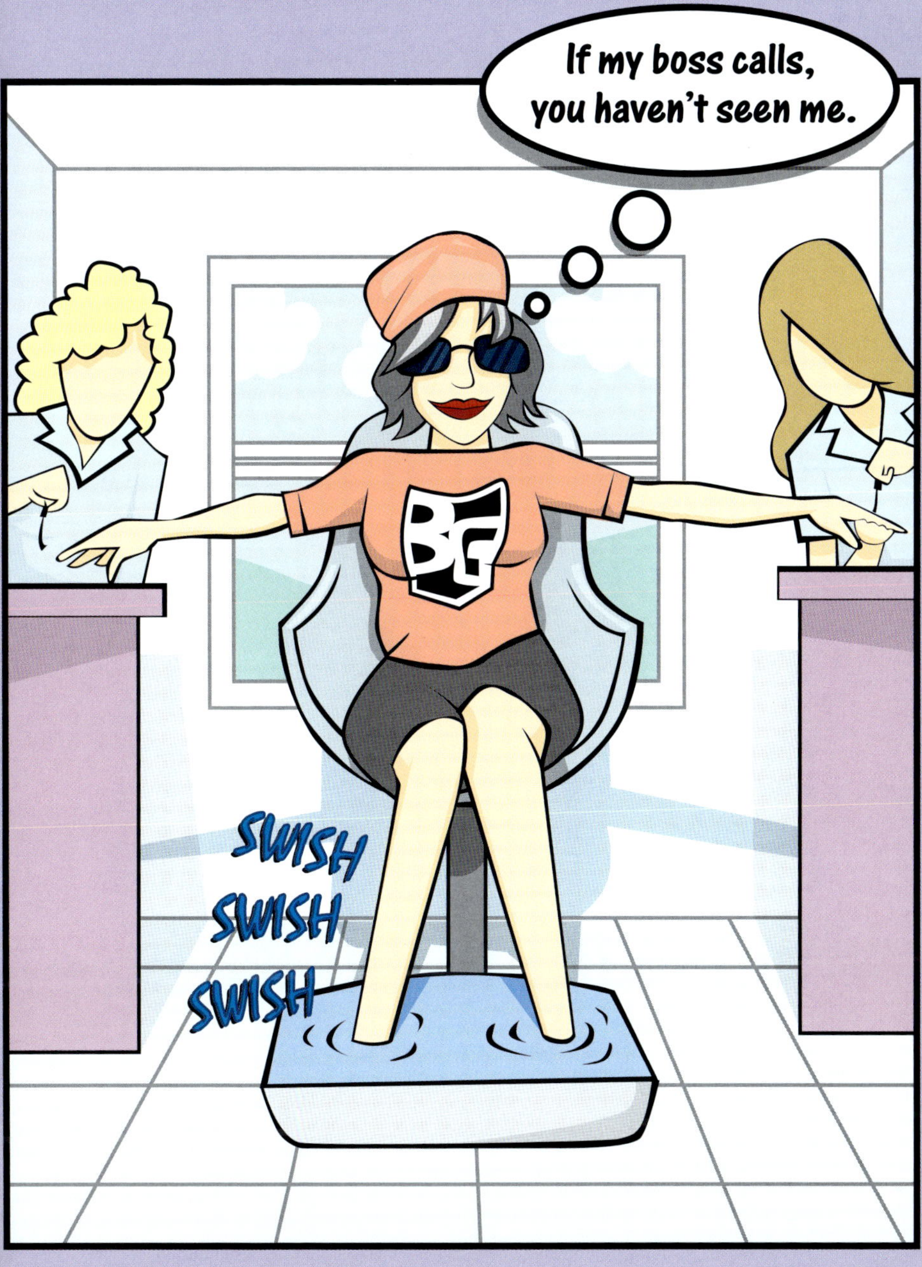
If my boss calls,
you haven't seen me.
SWISH
SWISH
SWISH

Boomer Girl burns a quick four hundred calories while catching up on world news, sipping a chai latte with skim, checking the afternoon forecast, and wailing with Aretha at the top of her lungs.

What you want . . . baby, I've got it . . . what you need . . . you know I've got it . . .
PEOPLE
CLOP!
CLOP!
CLOP!

A Black Belt in aikido, Boomer Girl defends her turf from aggressors like boomerang kids.

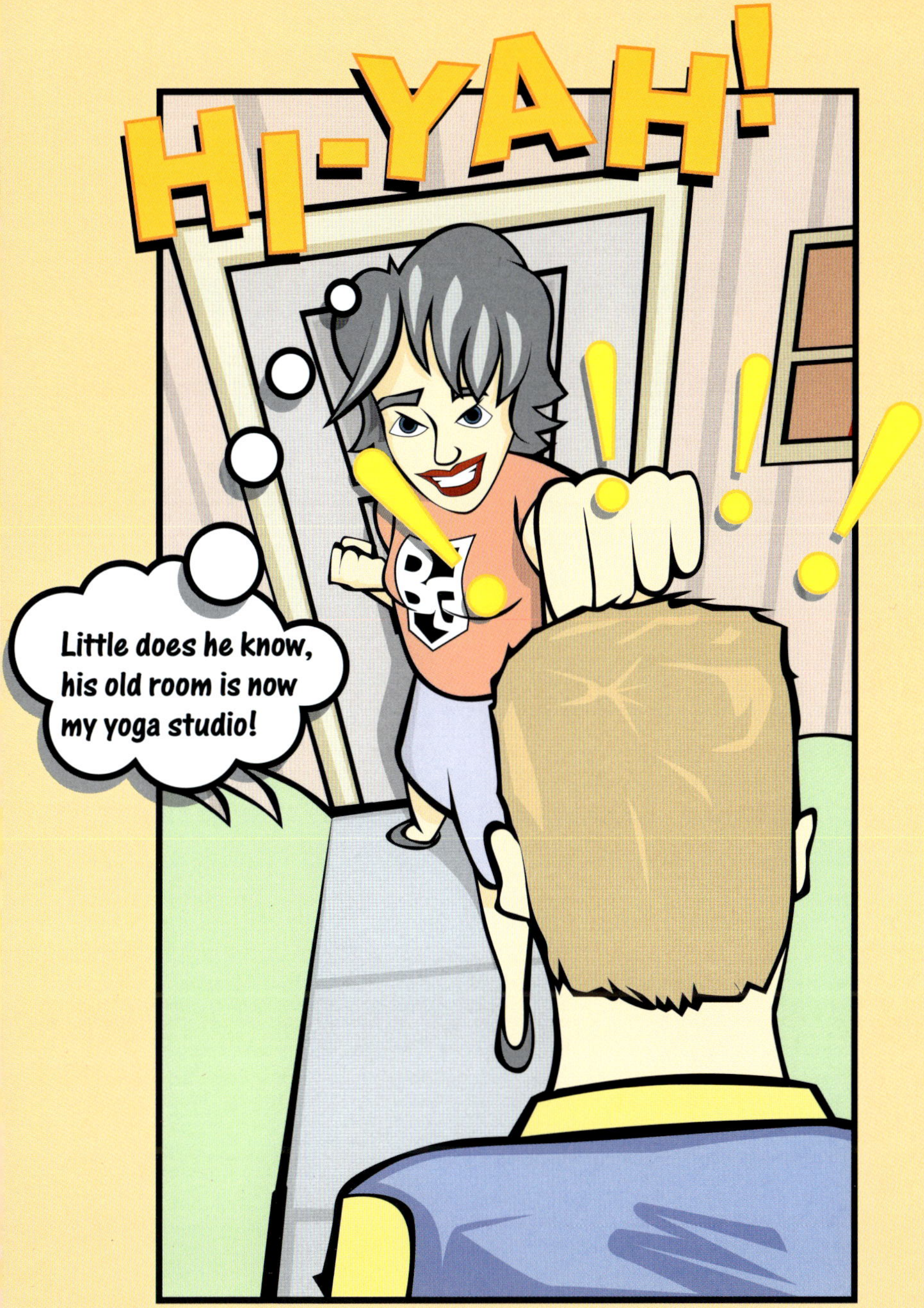
HI-YAH!
Little does he know, his old room is now my yoga studio!

With a wallet full of cash and a hot young stud in her crosshairs, Boomer Girl closes in and flirts shamelessly, just because she can.

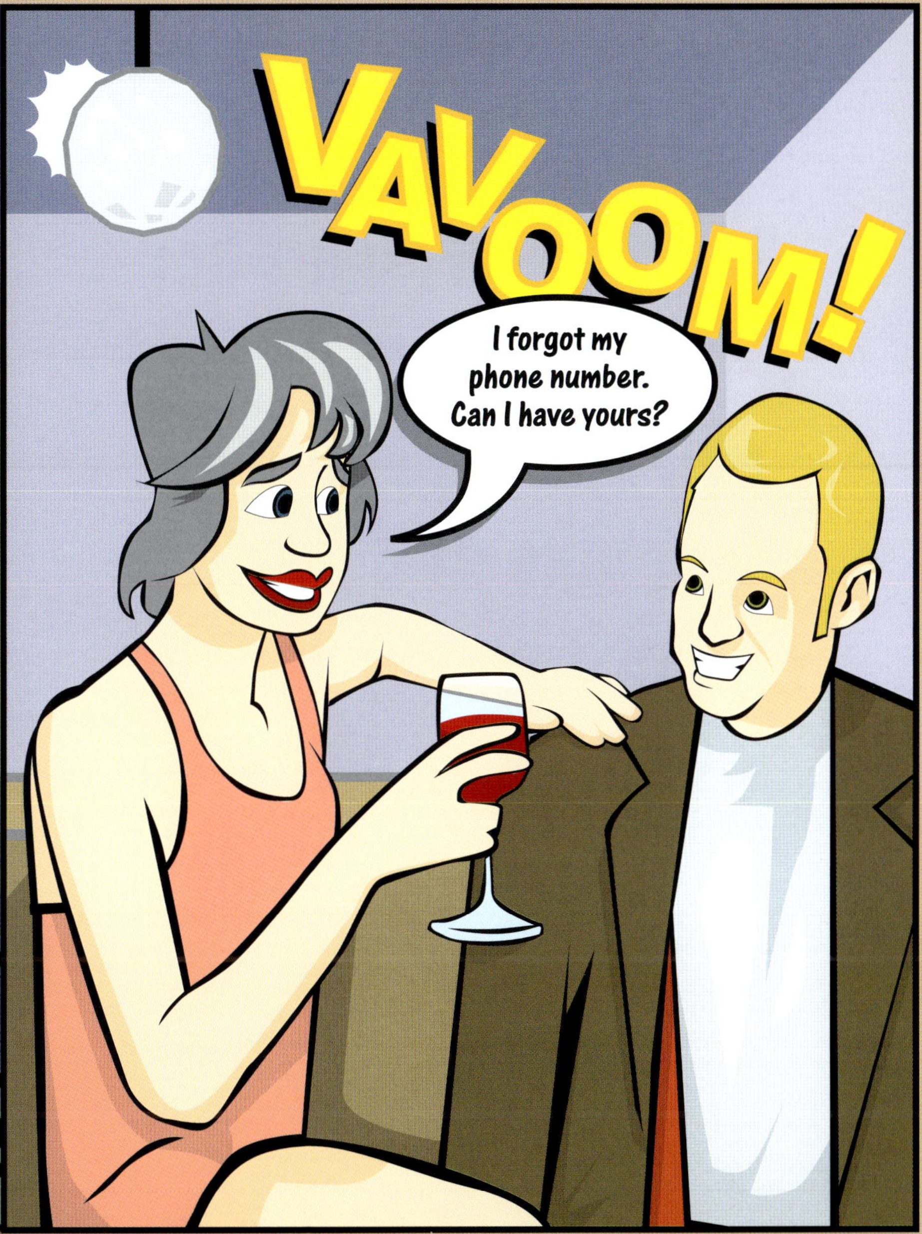
VAVOOM!
I forgot my phone number. Can I have yours?

Boomer Girl uses her X-ray vision to expose evil married men on the make and protect unsuspecting young women everywhere.

Thank you, Boomer Girl!

That's what I'm here for.

Boomer Girl never waits to be asked. 'Cause when you got it, you gotta shake it!

Her mission accomplished, at least for now, Boomer Girl gives herself a well-deserved reward.